WRITTEN AND
ILLUSTRATED BY

SIMON ABBOTT

Written and illustrated by Simon Abbott

Design by Collaborate Ltd.
Editor Becca Arlington
Designer Holly Green
Sensitivity Reader Lisa Davis
Jacket Coordinator Elin Woosnam
Managing Art Editor Elle Ward
Production Editor Gillian Reid
Senior Production Controller Leanne Burke
Publisher James Mitchem

First published in Great Britain in 2026 by
Dorling Kindersley Limited
20 Vauxhall Bridge Road,
London SW1V 2SA

The authorised representative in the EEA is
Dorling Kindersley Verlag GmbH. Arnulfstr. 124,
80636 Munich, Germany

Text and Illustration copyright © Simon Abbott 2026
Copyright © 2026 Dorling Kindersley Limited
A Penguin Random House Company
10 9 8 7 6 5 4 3 2 1
001–356279–May/2026

All rights reserved.
No part of this publication may be reproduced, stored in or introduced into
a retrieval system, or transmitted, in any form, or by any means (electronic,
mechanical, photocopying, recording, or otherwise), without the prior
written permission of the copyright owner.
No part of this publication may be used or reproduced in any manner for
the purpose of training artificial intelligence technologies or systems. In
accordance with Article 4(3) of the DSM Directive 2019/790, DK expressly
reserves this work from the text and data mining exception.

A CIP catalogue record for this book
is available from the British Library.
ISBN: 978-0-2417-9114-1

Printed and bound in China

www.dk.com

MIX
Paper | Supporting
responsible forestry
FSC™ C018179

This book was made with Forest
Stewardship Council™ certified
paper – one small step in DK's
commitment to a sustainable future.
**Learn more at www.dk.com/uk/
information/sustainability**

THE GREATEST MISTAKES IN HISTORY

CONTENTS

Page 6 — Chapter 1: Ridiculous Rulers

Page 13 — Chapter 2: Engineering Emergencies

Page 22 — Chapter 3: Blunders in Battle

Page 30 — Chapter 4: Awful Adventures

Page 37 — Chapter 5: Dead-end Discoveries

Page 47 — Chapter 6: Business Bungles

Page 58 — Chapter 7: Geographical Gaffes

Page 70 — Chapter 8: Excruciating Entertainment

Welcome to

THE GREATEST MISTAKES IN HISTORY!

If you feel **embarrassed** about
slipping on a banana skin,
muddling up your words,
forgetting your Great Aunt's birthday,
or **burning** the toast,
then this is the book for **you**!

Watch out!

Get ready to discover **mess-ups** and **bloopers** of epic proportions!

You'll read about historical **howlers** from ancient times and monumental **mix-ups** that are best left in the past.

Whatever **blunders** have left you blushing, you've got nothing on these **greatest gaffes of all time**!

Looks like I'm in a sticky situation!

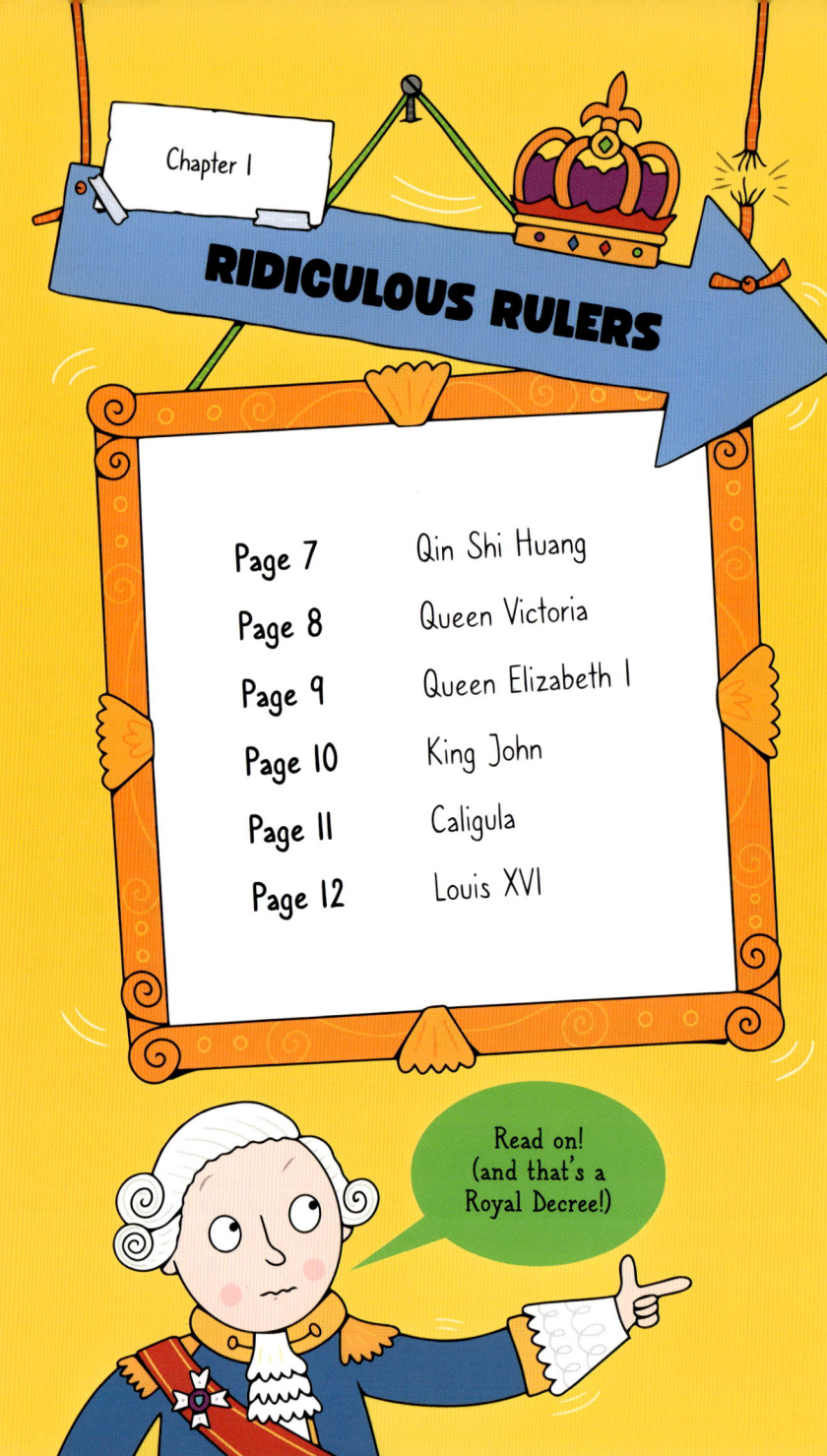

QIN SHI HUANG
THE IMMORTAL EMPEROR

Meet Qin Shi Huang, China's first emperor. He built 200 palaces, was limitlessly wealthy, and had an army of servants. But here's the plot twist: despite having literally everything, there was still one thing missing — he wanted to **live forever**!

Qin Shi Huang launched massive expeditions seeking the mythical "**islands of the immortals**" and hunted for magical herbs. Magicians whipped up special elixirs, which the emperor happily knocked back. Big mistake!

These "life-extending" cocktails were actually loaded with **mercury**. Rather than granting eternal life, these concoctions poisoned the poor emperor, which resulted in his death in 210 BCE, at just 49 years old.

We've got you covered, boss!

AFTERLIFE ARRANGEMENTS

Despite not living forever, Qin Shi Huang was more than ready for the afterlife. He had an enormous underground burial tomb built, which was guarded by 8,000 life-size clay soldiers and hundreds of chariots and horses known as the **Terracotta Army**.

QUEEN VICTORIA
CONFUSION AT THE CORONATION

When Queen Victoria was crowned in 1838 at **Westminster Abbey**, the ceremony was memorable for a series of unfortunate blunders.

Nobody seemed to know what was going on, and the queen had only visited the abbey the day before. The mishaps began when the **Archbishop of Canterbury** jammed the queen's ring on the wrong finger, and she had to soak her swollen digit in iced water to get it off! At one point, 82-year-old **Lord Rolle** climbed the steps to pledge loyalty to the newly-crowned Queen Victoria, but he took a tumble and fell down in a heap.

The ceremony dragged on for **five hours**, with members of the royal family popping out to a side chapel for wine and sandwiches! Finally, a confused bishop incorrectly told Queen Victoria that the ceremony was over, so she had to make a U-turn and sit herself down again!

FAST FACTS

LENGTH OF REIGN: Victoria became queen at 18 years old and spent 64 years on the throne.

FAMILY LIFE: She had 9 children, 42 grandchildren, and 87 great-grandchildren.

ROYAL TRAIN: In 1842, Victoria became the first monarch to travel by train.

We are NOT amused!

QUEEN ELIZABETH I
BESSIE'S BEAUTY TIPS

A dose of smallpox in 1562 left Queen Elizabeth I with scars on her face. Wanting to reduce their appearance, the queen decided to coat her face with a 2.5 cm (1 in) layer of make-up called **Venetian ceruse**.

What Elizabeth I didn't realize, was that the powder contained dangerous poisons, including **white lead**. Her skin began to deteriorate and her hair fell out. To make matters worse, she left the make-up on for at least a week, then took it off with a mixture containing another toxic poison called **mercury**.

The women who copied the queen didn't realize the mercury make-up remover was literally peeling away their skin.

What a majestic mess!

SOVEREIGN STATS

PARENTS: Elizabeth I was the daughter of King Henry VIII and Anne Boleyn.

FASHION FANATIC: She hoarded ornate clothes and owned thousands of gowns and gloves.

LANGUAGE LOVER: Elizabeth I was fluent in many languages.

KING JOHN
A (LITERALLY) LOUSY LOSER

King John wasn't exactly a people person. He made his nephew mysteriously "disappear", starved his friend's wife and son to death, assaulted his knights' daughters, feuded with the pope, and snatched lands from his priests.

In 1215, his barons revolted against his ruthless reign. They ordered him to sign a document called the **Magna Carta**, which limited his powers and forced him to follow rules... for once.

Still, the flare-up with his pesky barons grumbled on. The king sped to Lincolnshire to rally support, but made the ridiculous decision to cross a boggy estuary called **The Wash**. King John rode ahead, but his treasure wagons were caught by the rising tide. Silver plates, gold coins, goblets, jewels, and crowns were all swallowed by the waves. Poor King John wasn't embarrassed for too long, as he died of an illness called **dysentery** just eight days later on 19th October 1216.

Hey, Softsword! Coming to find you... ready or not!

SOVEREIGN SHOWDOWN

King John's elder brother was nicknamed "the Lionheart" due to his reputation for bold leadership and bravery. Meanwhile, John was known as "Softsword", as he had a habit of running away when the going got tough!

CALIGULA
A SEASIDE SKIRMISH

The Roman emperor Caligula was famous for his bizarre behaviour. In 40 CE, just three years into his reign, he decided to invade **Britain**. Rather than sail over the English Channel with boats full of fully-armed legionaries, Caligula declared war on **Neptune**, the god of the sea. He ordered his elite soldiers to stab the waves with their swords, then commanded them to fill their helmets with **seashells**. These were to be the "spoils of war" to be shown off in a full-blown victory parade back in Rome.

As a monument to this great "conquest", Caligula demanded that a lighthouse be built, which burned fires as a navigation aid for ships at night. One of his better ideas!

Everything's looking rosy!

ROMAN ROTTERS

Perhaps Caligula wasn't the worst Roman emperor, as Emperor **Elagabalus** hosted banquets with inedible food made from wood, stone, or wax to torment his guests! It's said he once dropped so many rose petals from the ceiling that several guests suffocated under the mountain of flowers.

LOUIS XVI
GETAWAY GAFFE

Louis XVI of France lived in lavish luxury at **Versailles**, a palace boasting 2,300 rooms, 67 staircases, 50 fountains, and a private village for the queen. In the real world, French workers were struggling with sky-high bread prices and unfair taxes. By 1789, they had officially had enough. **The French Revolution** demanded rights, freedom, and an end to the power of the royal family and their posh pals.

Time for the king to make a **low-key** getaway? Not exactly! Louis XVI tried to flee in a huge, bright yellow coach, complete with a pantry, cooker, and folding tables. His **footmen** were kitted out with fancy yellow uniforms, too! When the royal escapees stopped to change horses, a local postmaster took one look at Louis and recognized him from his profile on a coin. The king was swiftly arrested, and "**Louis the Last**" lost his head by the **guillotine**.

It's not bunny. I mean… funny!

BUNNY BONAPARTE

After the French Revolution, a man named Napoleon Bonaparte took power and put his brother on Holland's throne. His brother's Dutch was absolutely terrible – he accidentally announced to the entire nation that he was the "**Rabbit of Holland**" instead of the "**King of Holland**". Epic royal blunder!

THE FRENCH RAILWAY
COMMUTER CHAOS

France is incredibly proud of its **rail network**, which is the second largest in Europe. But imagine the embarrassment in 2014, when its train company ordered 2,000 brand new trains that were too wide for many of its platforms.

After spending **€15 billion** (£12.1 billion) on the oversized trains, they were faced with a **€50 million** (£40.6 million) bill to adapt many regional stations. The train company blamed the rail operator and said they were given the wrong dimensions... At least they're now back on track!

MAKING TRACKS

PULLING POWER: France's train company operates around 15,000 trains a day, for over 10 million passengers.

FIRST IN FRANCE: The first French railway opened in 1828, between Saint-Étienne and Andrézieux.

MISSION TO MARS
MEASUREMENT MIX-UP

Teamwork makes the dream work. But, when the USA's National Aeronautics and Space Administration (**NASA**) was building the **Mars Climate Orbiter** there was a serious lack of communication.

The orbiter launched in 1998, and all was well — the satellite flew 670 million km (416 million miles) in nine and a half months on a trouble-free journey to Mars. But disaster struck when it entered the planet's atmosphere at a lower altitude than planned. The Orbiter was crushed by the **atmospheric pressure** and disintegrated.

The problem? The navigation team's calculations had used **metres and millimetres**, and the construction team's data was in **feet** and **inches**. All that remained was a whopping £90 million space debris bill, and embarrassment all round!

SPACE DATES

On **12 April 1961**, Russian cosmonaut Yuri Gagarin became the ultimate space pioneer, whizzing around Earth in a spacecraft for 108 minutes.

On **20 July 1976**, Viking 1 became the first spacecraft to successfully land on Mars. It used a robotic arm to analyse soil samples and was hunting for signs of life (spoiler alert: none were found!).

THE SPANISH SUBMARINE
DEEP SEA DISASTER

In 2013, the Spanish Navy was excited about taking delivery of the *Isaac Peral*, a shiny, new, state-of-the-art **submarine**.

Instead, they were left with an expensive headache: an engineer on the **£1.75 billion** project had put a decimal point in the wrong place.

Number-crunching experts figured out that the vessel was 70 tonnes (77 tons) **too heavy** – it would have no problem getting to the bottom of the ocean, but coming up to the surface was a different matter. The navy had to dig deeper into their pockets for a **£9 million** fix-it fee!

SUB STATS

The **heaviest** submarine ever built is the Russian Typhoon-class. This super-sub measured **175 m (574 ft)**, tipped the scales at **43,500 tonnes (48,000 tons)**, and could cruise under the Arctic ice with its 160-person crew.

SS GREAT EASTERN
BOAT BLUNDER

Isambard Kingdom Brunel was one of the 19th century's most **talented engineers**. His crowning glory was to be the SS *Great Eastern*, an enormous steamship almost twice the length of a football pitch.

It was designed to carry **4,500 passengers, 6,000 tonnes (6,614 tons) of cargo**, and 12,000 tonnes (13,228 tons) of coal — enough fuel for a non-stop trip from the UK to India. Extra power came from sails, paddle wheels, and a propeller.

There was just one problem. The SS *Great Eastern* was **too big**! No dock or harbour could cope with its mammoth size, and its colossal hull couldn't squeeze through the brand-new Suez Canal. The ship's owners went broke, and the ship ended up as a cable-laying vessel, placing a permanent **telegraph link** between Europe and North America.

Spick and span!

FIRST AID FACTS

During the Crimean War, Isambard whipped up a ready-made hospital in just six days flat! The nursing legend Florence Nightingale gushed about Isambard's "magnificent huts" and their revolutionary focus on squeaky-clean hygiene.

THE MILLENNIUM BRIDGE
ROCK AND ROLL

What better way to celebrate the year 2000 than to open a sparkling, brand-new **bridge** over the River Thames: central London's first new crossing in **100 years**. Except the festivities didn't last long...

As crowds crossed the bridge, they experienced an alarming swaying motion, and as the bridge moved, pedestrians altered their steps to keep their balance. This action made the **Millennium Bridge** swing even more, and safety officials had to shut it down after just three days.

Quick-thinking engineers installed wobble-stopping devices called **dampers**, and the bridge reopened after nearly two years of closure.

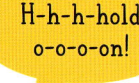

H-h-h-hold o-o-o-on!

FAST-FLOWING FACTS

ANCIENT ENGINEERING: Romans built the first bridge over the Thames almost **2,000 years ago**.

FROZEN FESTIVITIES: When the Thames froze solid, Londoners threw epic "frost fairs", with games, puppet shows, and souvenir shopping. The final fair in 1814 featured an **elephant** strutting its stuff across the frozen river.

RUSSIA'S RAILWAY
A BENDY BUNGLE

The all-powerful Tsar Nicholas I ruled **Russia** with super-strict control and authority. When he authorized the country's first major railway line between Moscow and Saint Petersburg in 1842, the tsar had a plan for the 650 km (404 mile) track.

Legend has it that when mapping out the route, Tsar Nicholas simply drew a **straight line** from one city to another. He accidentally traced around his own fingers, giving the track a bizarre bendy detour.

His nervous engineers were too terrified to point this out, so they built the railway to the **exact** royal route — including the imperial finger wobble!

One should always keep a cool head!

HAIR TODAY, GONE TOMORROW

Just like Tsar Nicholas I, Empress Elizabeth of Russia had some strict royal orders! She used a **heavy powder** to style her hair, as was the fashion in the 1700s. But when she was unable to wash it out and had to shave her head, she commanded all the other women at court to do the same, so she wasn't the odd one out!

FIRST FLIGHTS
AIRBORNE ANTICS

For centuries, humans have dreamed of flight, from ancient Chinese bamboo-copters, to Leonardo da Vinci's 15th century flying machines, to the Montgolfiers' hot air balloons in the 1780s. Early enthusiasts tried everything to take off: feathered wings, bat-shaped contraptions, parachute-landing aircraft, and pedalling pilots.

Flight pioneer Otto Lilienthal became the first person to successfully fly a **glider**. Sadly, in 1896, he lost control, fell 15 metres (49 feet), and broke his spine. Seven years later, aviator Samuel Langley designed a flying machine with a powerful engine. But twice the plane crashed into the **Potomac River** in the USA, breaking up as it left its launch catapult.

Just days later, the **Wright brothers** finally struck gold and nailed the first powered, controlled aeroplane flight!

Made it to Moscow!

SKY-HIGH STATISTICS

In 1930, **Amy Johnson** became the ultimate flying queen, as she was the first woman to fly solo from London to Australia. She smashed records flying to South Africa, Japan, and the USA, then became the first pilot to zoom from London to Moscow in under 24 hours!

THE TILTING TOWER
PROBLEMS IN PISA

During the 12th century, Pisa was a powerful Italian city with a mighty navy and booming shipping trade. To show off its status, the city's bigwigs decided to build a jaw-dropping free-standing **marble bell tower**.

Building began in 1173, but very soon it became obvious that something was wrong. The tower was **tilting**! Engineers hit pause for almost 100 years until someone had the bright idea of making the upper storeys taller on the leaning side (spoiler: this made things worse!). So, what was wrong?

Red flag alert – Pisa comes from the Greek word for "**marshy land**"! The soft, squishy soil on one side couldn't handle the building's weight, causing the foundation to sink unevenly. *Grosso problema*! (That's "big problem" for non-Italian speakers!)

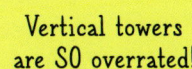

Vertical towers are SO overrated!

FACTS AND FIGURES

TICKETS PLEASE: Around **5 million tourists** flock to the Leaning Tower of Pisa every year.

STEP IT UP: There are **296 steps** to the top of the tower. Its tallest side is **56.67 m (186 ft) high** – around a sixth of the height of the Eiffel Tower.

KARÁNSEBES
AN AUSTRIAN OWN GOAL

In 1788, the 80,000-strong **Austrian army** was preparing for battle against the **Ottoman Empire**. The generals were plotting in Emperor Joseph II's tent, making a game plan for the Battle of Karánsebes.

Meanwhile, a boozy brawl broke out between a friendly Romanian unit and Austrian soldiers. And before they knew it...**BANG**! A shot was fired, sparking panic in the Austrian camp. Thinking that the shadowy figures in the dark were Ottoman soldiers, a confused Austrian commander gave the order for the cannons to fire, and in the chaos the great Austrian army fought to the death - **against themselves**!

When their actual enemy eventually strolled onto the scene, many Austrian soldiers had already been wiped out by **"friendly fire"** - an easy victory for the Ottoman Empire.

Willkommen zusammen! (Welcome, everybody!)

JOSEPH II FACT FILE

PARKS FOR THE PEOPLE: Joseph II opened Vienna's imperial hunting grounds and gardens to regular folks, earning him the nickname the **People's Emperor**.

AUSTRIAN A&E: In 1784, the emperor founded the **General Hospital** in Vienna, which, at the time, was one of Europe's biggest medical facilities.

STEDE BONNET
THE POINTLESS PIRATE

Stede Bonnet was a wealthy landowner from a posh English family in **Barbados**. Shockingly, he abandoned his wife, children, and fancy lifestyle to become a... pirate!

Stede had zero sailing know-how, but he blew his fortune buying a fancy ship and hiring a paid crew. This was a real no-no in piracy, as ships were usually stolen and crews were a mix of kidnapped sailors, escaped prisoners, and debt dodgers.

Stede Bonnet's piracy career was a **spectacular flop**. He relied fully on his crew for navigation and had his ship and supplies swiped by the fearsome pirate **Blackbeard**. In 1718, Stede sailed to North Carolina with a plan to relax during the hurricane season. Instead, the unlucky pirate was captured, tried, and sentenced to death (despite escaping for three weeks, supposedly in disguise!).

We're in the money!

A PIRATE PRIZE

In 1695, Henry Avery and his pirate crew ambushed a convoy of 25 ships owned by the **Mughal Empire**. The raiders made off with £600,000 in gold, silver, and precious stones – equal to £115 million today! Despite a whopping reward of £1,000 for his arrest, Henry Avery vanished forever – and so did the treasure!

THE TROJAN WAR
A GREEK MASTERPIECE

The Trojan War was a decade-long clash between the Ancient Greeks and the city of Troy. It kicked off in 1203 BCE when a Trojan prince ran off with Helen, the wife of the king of Sparta, an important city-state in Greece.

The Greeks clinched victory with a brilliant stunt. They built a colossal **wooden horse**, which they left outside Troy's gates, supposedly as an offering to the gods. They pretended to surrender and sail away, but secretly they had hidden their best fighters inside the hollow horse.

The Trojans were tricked. They hauled the horse inside the city and began their victory party. **BIG MISTAKE!** As darkness fell, the Greek elite force climbed out, unlocked the city gates, and let in their comrades. Troy had fallen!

SPARTAN STATISTICS

STARTING YOUNG: Spartan boys endured intense military training from the age of seven. They were finally allowed to retire from service at 60.

SPORT FOR ALL: Spartan girls were trained in wrestling, running, and horseback riding. In 396 BCE, a Spartan **princess**, became the first woman to win an **Olympic event**, having trained her horses for the chariot race.

HANNIBAL
RIVAL TO THE ROMANS

Hannibal was a brilliant military mastermind who used slick tactics to wipe out **Roman armies**. In 218 BCE, he plotted a daring mission — to complete the long trek from Spain to the heart of the Roman Empire in Italy. But there was one thing in the way — the Alps, Europe's highest mountain range.

He commanded an army of 38,000 foot soldiers, 8,000 troops on horseback, 15,000 mules and horses, and 37 **war elephants**! At first, the elephants were petrified of crossing the River Rhône but they were coaxed onto wooden rafts. Then they faced a freezing 16-day trail through snowy mountains. When Hannibal reached northern Italy, only a few elephants remained — just in time for the harsh Italian winter.

The lesson of this story? Don't plan an attack in glacial conditions over a treacherous mountain range using animals that are more at home in the **tropics**!

My trunk's gone numb!

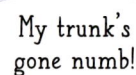

FIGHTING FACTS

Elephants aside, Hannibal's journey across the **Alps** was a military success, as by crossing a supposed impassable obstacle, he caught the Romans off guard. This element of surprise allowed Hannibal to score some early wins, including the **Battle of Ticinus** and the **Battle of the Trebbia River**.

SHOICHI YOKOI
LONG-LOST SOLDIER

In 1944, towards the end of WWII, American forces seized control of **Guam**, an island in the western Pacific Ocean.

Terrified of being captured, Japanese army sergeant **Shoichi Yokoi** fled into the jungle — and hid for 27 years! He survived on frogs, toads, river eels, and rats, then foraged for fruit and nuts. Using his pre-war skills as a **tailor**, Shoichi Yokoi wove clothing from tree bark and camouflaged his shelter with reeds and bamboo.

In 1972, two hunters discovered the long-lost soldier, who was embarrassed to find out that the war had ended **three decades** earlier. Shoichi Yokoi was given a hero's welcome on his return to Japan!

Bang! Pop! Kapow!

DID YOU KNOW?

FEEL THE BURN: Shoichi found that lighting a fire by rubbing bamboo sticks together was exhausting, so he added a pinch of gunpowder at just the right moment!

ALL-ROUNDERS: Ancient Japanese warriors, or samurai, weren't just skilled in combat — they mastered literature, flower arranging, rock gardening, and tea ceremonies, too!

TSUSHIMA
A BRUISING BATTLE

In 1905, Russia and Japan were at war, and the **Russian Navy** sent their fleet 30,000 km (18,600 miles) to fight it out with the **Japanese Navy**. During this seven-month voyage, ships crashed into each other, some ran aground and couldn't move, and others opened fire on **British fishing boats** when the Russians mistook them for Japanese torpedo boats. The crew contained huge numbers of untrained (and seasick) Russian sailors, and the poor conditions on board led to disease, exhaustion, and revolt.

By the time they came face to face with their enemy, the Russian sailors were ready to drop. 30 out of 36 Russian ships were sunk or captured — an all-out **victory** for the Japanese.

Hit!

FIREPOWER FACT

The **Battle of Tsushima** was the first major naval battle that used **wireless telegraphy** (radio). This allowed the Japanese to plot accurate locations of Russian ships, despite thick fog and poor visibility.

THE GREAT ESCAPE
FLUFFING THE FLIGHT TO FREEDOM

Throughout WWII, the Nazis used **Colditz Castle** as a prisoner-of-war camp. They thought that the hilltop location, steep cliffs, and thick walls made the castle escape-proof.

However, British officer **Michael Sinclair** wanted to prove them wrong. He planned to impersonate a German soldier and sneak out of Colditz undetected. For months, he studied Sergeant Major Gustav Rothenberger, mimicking his walk, mannerisms, routine, and accent. Michael sewed a uniform from **blankets**, crafted medals using **zinc** from the roof, and faked a pistol holder from **cardboard** and **boot polish**. He created the major's distinct moustache from a **shaving brush**!

In September 1943 the escape day came, only for Michael to end up at Gustav Rothenberger's feet – the guard he had been trying to imitate! Back to the drawing board...

We've made it to Berlin, lads!

GOOD-FOR-NOTHING GUARDS

Following a prison camp breakout, four German WWII escapees pinched a getaway car. They failed to start the car, so were given a push-start by their clueless **British guards** who mistook the runaways for mechanics!

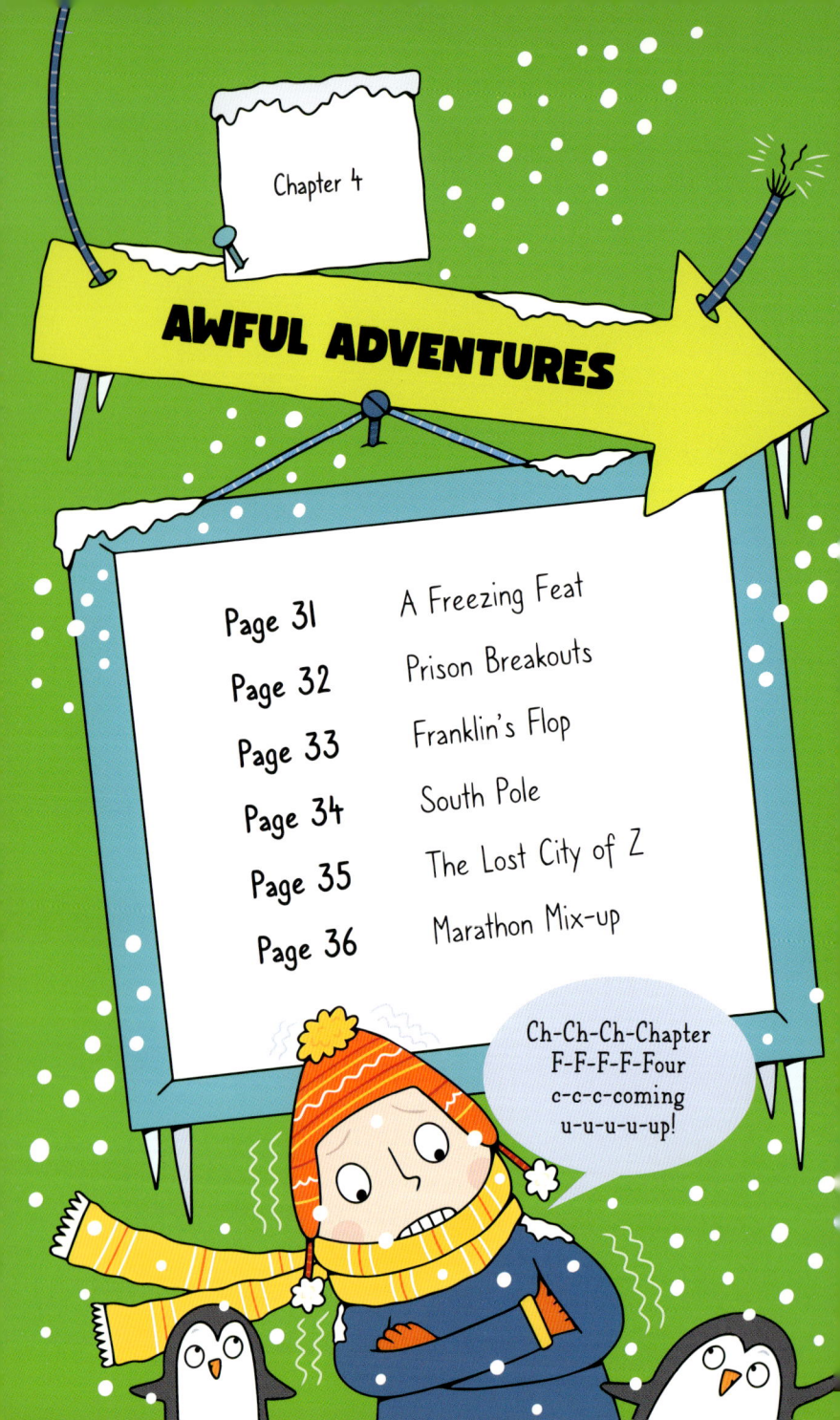

A FREEZING FEAT
HOT AIR IN THE ARCTIC

Here's an idea: rather than trekking to the bone-chilling North Pole on foot, why not try to view it from the air?

That was the brainchild of Swedish engineer **Salomon August Andrée** in 1897. He packed **The Eagle** gas balloon with scientific gear, cameras, and provisions, and took off with his friends Knut Frænkel and Nils Strindberg on board. Trouble began straight away. The balloon was too heavy so they hurled supplies and sandbags overboard, making The Eagle impossible to steer. The uncontrollable balloon landed after two days. The trio survived but were stranded in freezing Arctic wasteland. They hunted polar bears to pad out their meagre rations, as most food supplies had been thrown overboard.

The explorers headed south but read their maps incorrectly. They camped on an **ice floe**, hoping to float southwards, but fled when the ice began to crack.

There goes the frozen yoghurt!

END OF THE ADVENTURE

Their **diary entries** mysteriously stopped on 8 October 1897. Over 30 years later, the remains of the three men were found, complete with Nils' camera, photo reels, diaries, and the expedition boat.

PRISON BREAKOUTS
IT'S ALL IN THE DETAILS

Prisoner **James Edward Russell** was serving his fourth prison sentence when he decided to have a change of scene. In 2011, after landing at a low-security prison in Washington, USA, he made a break for it and ran like the wind (spoiler alert: he forgot to grab civilian clothes or arrange a getaway car!).

James sprinted for an impressive 22.5 km (14 miles) and found refuge in the surrounding woods. Spotting a **cozy cabin**, the genius escapee knocked politely to borrow the phone. The door swung open revealing... an **off-duty prison guard** from — you've guessed it — the prison he had just escaped from!

One look at James's bright red prison-issue uniform, and the game was up!

I knew that yoga class would come in handy!

THE KOREAN HOUDINI

Yoga expert Choi Gap-bok turned his bendy skills to good use when he was jailed on suspicion of robbery. He covered himself in ointment and squeezed through the tiny food slot in his cell door. The slippery suspect was locked up after six days of freedom — with a tinier food slot!

FRANKLIN'S FLOP
NORTHWEST PASSAGE NO-NO

Countless seafarers throughout history have had one goal in mind: conquering the legendary **Northwest Passage** connecting the Atlantic and Pacific oceans and creating a money-making trade route to Asia.

With this in mind, the polar explorer **Captain Sir John Franklin** sailed to northern Canada in May 1845. He commanded two powerful ships, HMS *Erebus* and HMS *Terror*. They were equipped with hot-water heating, live cattle, pigs and hens, libraries with over 1,000 books, and a three-year supply of tinned food.

In late July, while waiting to be freed by the Arctic ice, Captain John's two ships were spotted by a whaling ship. Sadly, this was the final sighting of all 129 crew members.

WHAT HAPPENED?

After being stuck in ice for a bone-chilling **19 months**, the crew deserted the ships in 1848, having endured starvation, scurvy, and hypothermia. However, recent research points the finger at deadly **lead poisoning**. Could the expedition's food have been **contaminated** by the lead solder used to seal the tins?

SOUTH POLE
A SPRINT IN THE SNOW

In 1911, rival **British** and **Norwegian** explorers Robert Scott and Roald Amundsen were racing to be the first to reach the South Pole.

Robert's preparation has been criticized. His team wore damp woollen gear, while Roald's crew sported warm **reindeer skins**. Robert's ponies slipped in the powdery snow and his motorized sledges broke down, forcing the crew to drag the heavy supplies. The Norwegian crew used **dog sleds** and skis.

While Roald's Greenland dogs were given fresh meat, many of Robert's dogs went hungry due to a supply of rotten food. The British were further delayed by brutal blizzards and miscommunication. Unsurprisingly, Roald's team was triumphant and they raised the **Norwegian flag** at the South Pole on 14 December 1911. A month later, a bitterly disappointed Robert arrived to take second place.

Medium rare, please, Roald!

ANTARCTIC FACT FILE

Antarctica is a polar desert, receiving around 150 mm (6 in) of water each year, usually in the form of snow. It is capped by an ice sheet **4.8 km (3 miles) thick**. Around 10,000 scientists work there in the summer, dropping to **1,000 (freezing) experts** during the winter months!

THE LOST CITY OF Z
AMAZON ADVENTURES

British explorer **Percy Fawcett** was obsessed with finding an ancient city he called **Z**, deep in the **Amazon rainforest**. He had made seven attempts to locate the settlement, and had survived vampire bats, piranhas, flesh-eating maggots, poison-arrow attacks, and near-starvation in doing so.

His adventures had left him penniless, but a determined Percy eventually raised new funds for an eighth expedition, and splashed out on tinned food, powdered milk, guns, flares, mosquito nets, and a **ukulele**! He set off in April 1925, accompanied by his son Jack and his friend Raleigh Rimmel.

After writing a letter to his wife from **"Dead Horse Camp"** on 29 May, Percy Fawcett and his companions mysteriously vanished forever.

WHAT HAPPENED NEXT?

In an incredible plot twist, it turns out that Percy may have stumbled upon the **lost city** without realizing it. He had puzzled over shards of pottery that he'd unearthed on a previous trip. Researchers now believe that his find was the location of an enormous and sophisticated civilization, home to around **50,000 people**.

MARATHON MIX-UP
TAKING THE WRONG ROUTE

Halfway through the 2017 **Venice Marathon**, the race was super-tight, with very little separating the leading six runners. That was until their motorcycle escort accidentally messed up and turned off the planned route.

The elite pack took a wrong turn and sprinted behind the mixed-up motorcycle rider, following him for several hundred metres down a motorway ramp.

This was fantastic news for local Venetian runner **Eyob Faniel**, who knew the route back to front. He happily dashed past the top athletes and became the first Italian to win the race for 22 years!

Tieniti forte!
(Hold on tight!)

FLOATING FACTS

CITY OF CANALS: Venice is built on a network of islands and canals. It is home to 417 bridges and 350 boats called **gondolas**.

HIGH TIDE: Wobbly Venice is **sinking** a small amount every year.

SKINNY STREETS: Venice is **car-free**. Its narrowest street is just 53 cm (21 in) wide – imagine three and a half hotdogs end-to-end!

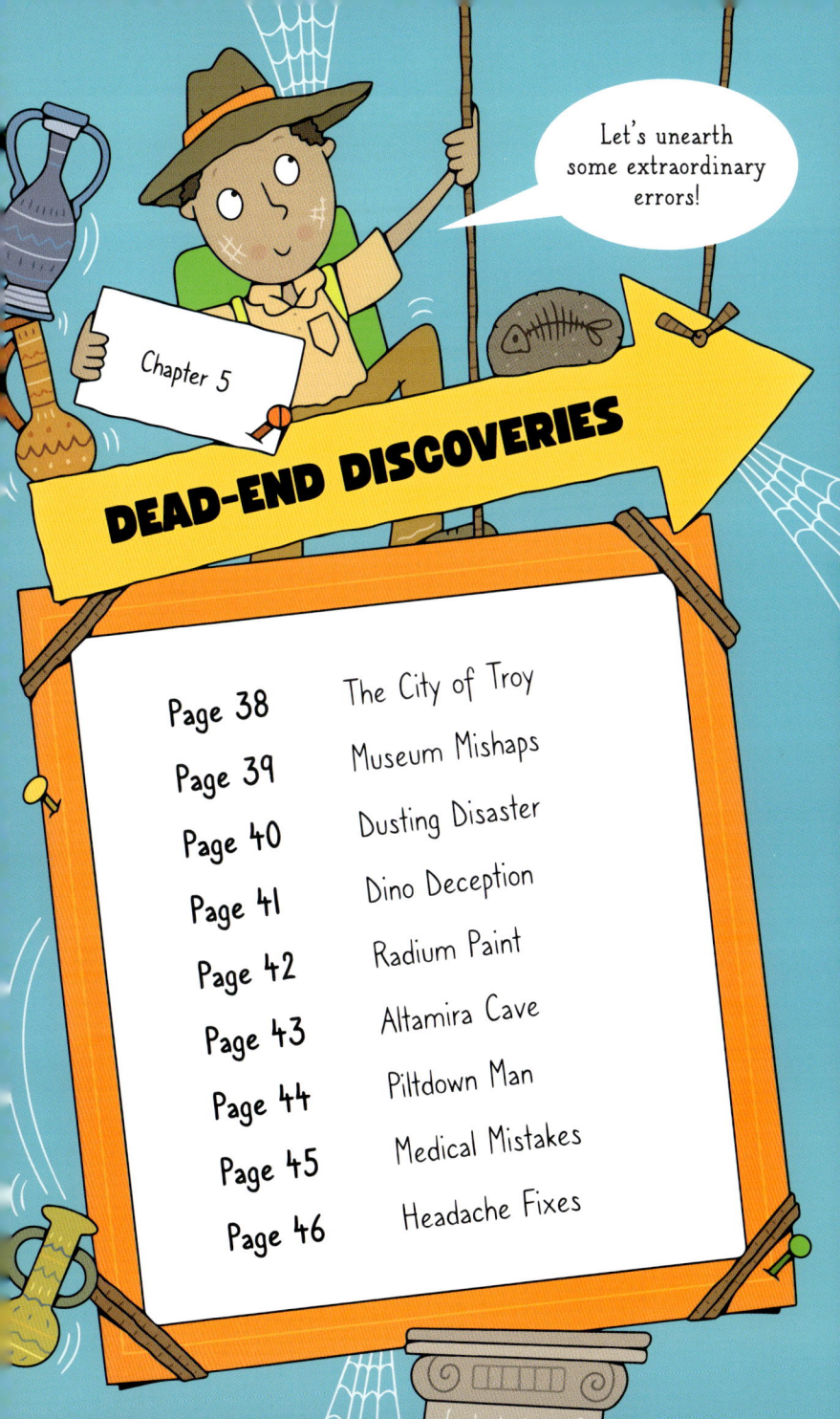

THE CITY OF TROY
EXTREME EXCAVATION

Heinrich Schliemann was a **treasure-hunting fanatic**! He had spent years dreaming of discovering the lost city of Troy, so when a possible location in Turkey was identified in the 1870s, he just couldn't wait to get started!

Heinrich ordered his crew to dig a **massive trench**, deeper than three stacked double decker buses. They shovelled their way through layers of rock and soil without taking records or mapping ancient finds.

He used dynamite to speed up the process, blowing up historical remains, valuable artifacts, and fragile archaeological secrets. The top layers Heinrich had tossed aside as worthless rubble? They were probably his prize — the **ancient city of Troy!**

5...4...3...2...oops...!

DIGGING DATA

DUSTY DEALS: Heinrich struck it rich selling **gold dust** in America.

CLEVER COMMUNICATION: Heinrich boasted that he could master languages in just **six weeks**! He could chat away in (take a breath) English, French, Dutch, Spanish, Portuguese, Italian, Russian, Swedish, Polish, Greek, Latin, and Arabic, plus his native German!

MUSEUM MISHAPS
CRASH, BANG, WALLOP

Have you ever tripped over your shoelaces?

Well, picture the visitor to the UK's **Fitzwilliam Museum** who went tumbling down a staircase in 2006. He tripped, fell, and smashed not one, not two, but three **Qing Dynasty** vases.

Result? An epic **£500,000** bill – and the world's biggest pottery jigsaw puzzle!

I'm having a smashing time!

FINE ART FIASCO

That same year, chaos struck during an art class at New York's **Metropolitan Museum of Art**. One wobbly student lost her balance and toppled into a painting. But this was no ordinary doodle! We're talking about **Picasso's** masterpiece *The Actor*, worth a jaw-dropping £75 million. The 15 cm (6 in) tear got an emergency repair from the super-skilled conservation department, and it took pride of place in the museum's Picasso exhibition four months later.

DUSTING DISASTER
SCRUBBED AND SPOILED

An eager cleaner at the **Ostwall Museum** in Germany was unhappy about marks on a modern art installation, so scrubbed away at the stain until it sparkled. Unfortunately, the mark was a deliberate part of artist Martin Kippenberger's sculpture, **When It Starts Dripping From the Ceiling**, meant to look like a dried rain puddle.

The art piece was on loan to the museum and was worth a mere **£690,000**. The museum had given strict instructions for staff to stay at least 20 cm (8 in) away from the exhibits, but maybe this cleaner had a particularly long scrubbing brush!

That's better!

THUMBS UP

Do you remember Qin Shi Huang's 2,000-year-old **Terracotta Army** from China? It was being exhibited at the Franklin Institute in Philadelphia, when a visitor snuck in, snapped a selfie with a £3 million statue, and snapped off its thumb. The Chinese were livid, and the culprit was slapped with a £7,500 fine (and had to hand back the souvenir stolen digit!).

DINO DECEPTION
FOSSIL FRAUD

In 1999, explosive news rocked the dinosaur world. Chinese farmers had unearthed a spectacular **Archaeoraptor**. This turkey-sized specimen had the tail of a dinosaur and the arms of a primitive bird. It was hailed as the **missing link**, connecting these two groups.

This valuable specimen got snapped up by a museum for £60,000, but when the fossil was X-rayed, red flags were raised. The creature had been assembled from **88 different pieces of stone and fossil**. Half belonged to an ancient bird, the other half to a vicious raptor, but it had tricked some of the world's smartest scientists!

Fossilized fool!

Prehistoric pinhead!

THE BONE WARS

In the 19th century, a ruthless **rivalry** grew between two dinosaur hunters, Edward Drinker Cope and Othniel Charles Marsh. It kicked off when Othniel mocked Edward for mixing up an Elasmosaurus's neck and tail, after he stuck the specimen's head on the wrong end!

Their jealousy was petty, but it drove both men to uncover a **huge number of new dinosaurs** (although their hurry did lead to sloppy mistakes in identifying and naming them).

RADIUM PAINT
WATCH WARNING

In the early 20th century, **watchmakers** discovered that if their watch dials were coated in **radium paint** they would glow in the dark. Talk about a unique selling point!

The talented women who carried out this precise work were encouraged to use their lips to keep their fine-tipped brushes in tip-top shape. There was just one problem — radium paint was **radioactive**. Every time the workers licked their brushes, they swallowed a tiny dose of radioactive material.

HOW DID THIS AFFECT THEM?

Dentists first spotted the horrifying health issues experienced by dial painters, as one by one they experienced wobbly teeth, ulcers, and a painful "radium jaw". The brave **Radium Girls** took their bosses to court and won a yearly payment for life.

Their legal case gained momentum when the paint's actual inventor, Dr von Sochocky, suffered from exposure to radium himself.

ALTAMIRA CAVE
A SERIOUS SMUDGE

In 1879, amateur archaeologist Marcelino Sanz de Sautuola was poking around Spain's **Altamira Cave**. He'd dragged along his eight-year-old daughter, Maria, who soon ran off to explore. Suddenly, she glanced up and shouted, "*Mira Papa! Bueyes pintados!*" (Meaning, "Look Dad! Painted oxen!")

Marcelino was convinced that this incredible collection of cave masterpieces were genuine **Palaeolithic** art treasures — creations dating back roughly **15,000 years**! His findings were ridiculed by professional archaeologist Émile Cartailhac who sent his colleague, Édouard Harlé, to disprove the evidence. When he arrived, Édouard believed that the cave paintings were fake because the colours were so vibrant and well-preserved!

WHAT HAPPENED NEXT?

In 1902, **Émile Cartailhac** finally visited Altamira Cave and was blown away by the **ancient art**. He knew that he had made a **monumental blunder**. He published an article to reverse his original scientific judgement and issued a heartfelt apology to the late Marcelino for ruining his reputation!

C'est faux!
(It's fake!)

PILTDOWN MAN
SKULL SLIP-UPS

Charles Dawson was a super-keen amateur **archaeologist**, with noteworthy finds including three new dinosaur species, a Roman statuette, a Stone Age axe, and an ancient boat.

He donated his prized fossil finds to the **Natural History Museum** in London, who gave him the title of "honorary collector". So, when Charles claimed to have unearthed the **missing link** between apes and humans in 1912, experts in the natural world went wild with excitement!

Arthur Smith Woodward, a bigwig at the Natural History Museum, jumped onboard and together they reconstructed a skull using the teeth, jawbone, and bone fragments Charles had discovered. They were convinced that their ground-breaking evidence pointed to a 500,000-year-old ancestor, nicknamed the "**Piltdown Man**"!

Let's play fake or fossil!

ACCURATE ANALYSIS

Fast forward almost 40 years and state-of-the-art **technology** proved that the remains were only 50,000 years old. "Piltdown Man" was a mishmash of a modern human skull, an orangutan's jawbone, and ape-like teeth filed down to make them look human. X-rays revealed that putty had secured the teeth, and the fragments had been aged with paint. What a hoax!

MEDICAL MISTAKES
PUZZLING PILLS AND POTIONS

History is packed with ridiculous remedies and medical mishaps. Europeans in the 18th century genuinely believed that crushed-up **Egyptian mummies** possessed healing powers. As demand grew, grave robbers started producing fake mummies by drying out the corpses of freshly executed criminals.

Can you guess what a **"tobacco smoke enema"** was? It involved blowing tobacco smoke up a patient's bottom to revive them and was thought to work brilliantly on victims of drowning. In the 1780s, emergency kits containing special bellows were dotted along the River Thames in London.

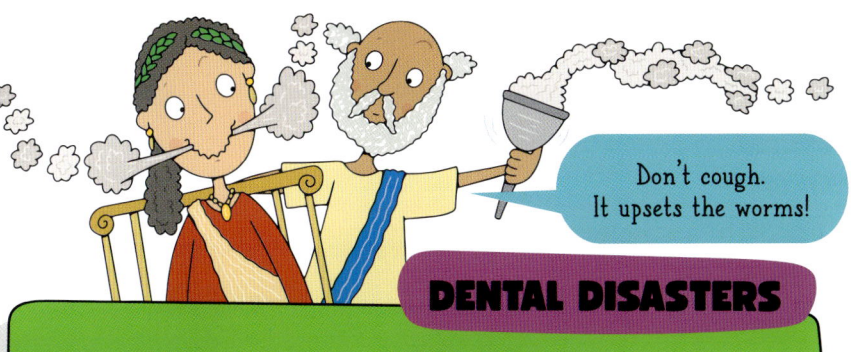

Don't cough. It upsets the worms!

DENTAL DISASTERS

As far back as 5,000 BCE, it was thought that tiny worms caused **toothache**. Doctors would burn plants and seeds and, using a funnel, would waft smoke into the sufferer's mouth to coax the "worm" out of the rotten tooth. Ash from the burnt seeds looked like worms, which convinced the patient that the treatment had been a success!

HEADACHE FIXES
ROMAN REMEDIES

Throbbing heads are relieved today with a simple tablet. Historically, doctors drilled holes in patients' skulls to cure headaches, and they did this for epilepsy and depression, too. This procedure dates back to Stone Age times, with evidence to suggest that many patients survived this terrifying ordeal.

Ancient Roman headache cures were slightly better — crushed **snails** smeared across the forehead! Romans patched up wounds and bruises with **wild boar poo**, and soothed burns by mixing burnt goat poo, olive oil, and sugar. Acne was treated with **crocodile meat**, or sufferers could bathe in oil and sour cheese. A blend of basil and boot polish was prescribed to remove warts and stop constant farting — but exceeding the dose could put someone in a coma!

There's success in slime!

A MESSY MIRACLE

Dramatic discoveries are sometimes found in messy mistakes! In 1928, Alexander Fleming went on holiday, leaving dirty petri dishes in his lab. He returned, peered into the dishes, and spotted a fuzzy mould, which turned out to be a substance that killed bacteria. He called it **penicillin**. This medical miracle went into production in 1942, treating infections such as pneumonia.

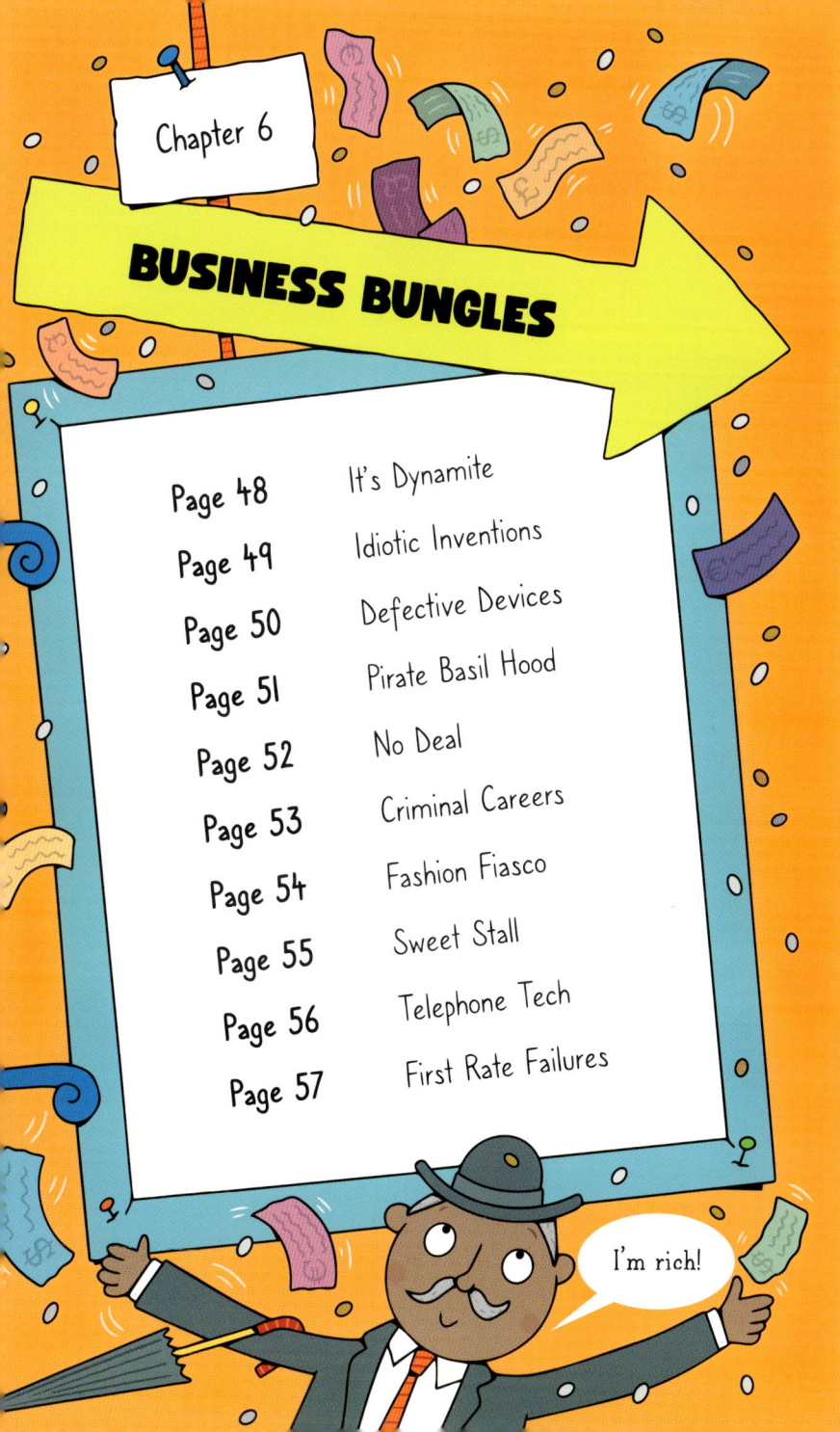

Chapter 6

BUSINESS BUNGLES

Page 48	It's Dynamite
Page 49	Idiotic Inventions
Page 50	Defective Devices
Page 51	Pirate Basil Hood
Page 52	No Deal
Page 53	Criminal Careers
Page 54	Fashion Fiasco
Page 55	Sweet Stall
Page 56	Telephone Tech
Page 57	First Rate Failures

I'm rich!

IT'S DYNAMITE
AN EXPLOSIVE EXPERIMENT

Alfred Nobel was a brainy boffin — a chemist, businessman, engineer, and inventor. He trained in chemistry, becoming fascinated with a highly explosive liquid called **nitroglycerine**.

Alfred experimented to see if it could be used in the building industry, but then disaster struck! He blew up his laboratory, along with several scientists and his brother, Emil.

This tragedy didn't stop him. In 1866, Alfred discovered that if nitroglycerine was mixed with **sand**, it could be shaped into rods and stuck inside drilled holes. He called this new invention **dynamite**. His **detonator** guaranteed a controlled blast and commercial demand for dynamite "exploded"!

Ms Morrison, your book is DYNAMITE!

NOBEL'S LEGACY

Alfred donated most of his 31 million Swedish kronor fortune (around £150 million in today's money) to create the **Nobel Prizes** — awards that honour outstanding contributions to humankind. Previous winners include the pioneering scientist **Marie Curie** (for chemistry and physics), the acclaimed novelist **Toni Morrison** (for literature), and the courageous education activist **Malala Yousafzai** (for peace).

IDIOTIC INVENTIONS
CATASTROPHIC CREATIONS

Meet tailor (and eager entrepreneur) Franz Reichelt. Inspired by the advances in flight, in 1912 he designed an impressive **parachute suit** for pilots. After trial runs using dummies, Franz was **positive** his invention would be a hit. He leaped from The Eiffel Tower in Paris, but sadly, the suit failed, and Franz was wiped out in a few seconds flat.

Another irresponsible invention came from a Victorian parents' manual, which recommended that babies have plenty of fresh air. This inspired the **baby cage**, which parents could suspend from a window, pop the infant inside, and enjoy some peace! It was popular in apartment blocks and, **amazingly**, no safety issues were reported. Phew!

My business is in freefall!

ANTI-BURGLAR BRIEFCASE

Imagine a briefcase designed to bamboozle a burglar. If snatched, "The Arrestor" case set off a loud alarm, the handle trapped the thief's fingers, and three super-long metal poles shot out, making it impossible to escape through a doorway or by getaway car!

DEFECTIVE DEVICES
GOOD-FOR-NOTHING GIZMOS

Do you think a cat could be transformed into a snooping **super-spy**? In the 1960s, the CIA (the USA's foreign intelligence service) launched **Operation Acoustic Kitty**.

It took five years and $20 million (over £15 million) to create a high-tech cat! It had a tiny transmitter and microscopic microphone for recording classified conversations throughout the **Russian government**.

Finally, it was ready to test. But on its first trip out, the cat crossed the street and was hit by a taxi. Mission aborted.

The name's Dragon... Dragonfly Drone!

INSECT INVENTION

The CIA didn't give up. It switched from furry secret agents to insect intelligence, developing a miniature **dragonfly drone** equipped with a small engine and fluttering wings. It was steered by a **laser beam** and transmitted secret chat back to the operator. Unfortunately, this dragonfly dud malfunctioned in windy weather.

PIRATE BASIL HOOD
DANGER ON DECK

Pirates are notorious for targeting treasure ships. Good profit! Good business! But **Basil Hood** was a pirate with a twist. Why risk a tussle with a heavily-armed vessel? Why not plan a raid with a difference?

Under cover of darkness, he dropped his anchor, marched to a farm, and captured... a field full of cows! Basil and his motley crew herded the confused beasts onboard, and then fled. All too soon, the pirates realized that treasure is far easier to control. The cows became horribly seasick and the stench could be smelt for **miles**.

In desperation, Basil's crew surrendered to a passing **British Naval ship**. The officers took one sniff and left the pongy pirates to it – and they refused to confiscate the cargo!

PASTEURIZED PETS

Speaking of cows, Cuban leader **Fidel Castro** had an ingenious idea to help his hard-up citizens. He asked his scientists to create **dog-sized cows**. They'd be small enough to live in a home, provide milk for the whole family, and feed on grass grown in drawers under fluorescent lights. A Fidel Fiasco!

NO DEAL
A SMALL BITE OF THE APPLE

On 1 April 1976, Steve Jobs, Steve Wozniak, and Ronald Wayne launched **Apple Computer Company**.

To fund their wild venture, Steve Jobs cashed in his beloved **camper van** and Steve Wozniak sold his precious **HP-65 calculator**. It was all systems go as they assembled the first batch of computers in Steve Jobs' parents' garage.

11 days later, Ronald Wayne wanted out, concerned about the rollercoaster nature of their start-up company. He banked **$800 (£590)** from his **10% share**. Today, with over 50 million iPads and 200 million iPhones sold each year, Ronald's split would be worth an eye-watering **$300 billion (£221 billion)**. You win some, you lose some!

STRATOSPHERIC SEARCH ENGINE

In 1998, Larry Page and Sergey Brin offered to sell their tiny start-up, called **Google**, to **Yahoo** for **$1 million**. They were turned down flat. Today, Google is worth an absolutely astronomical **$2.8 trillion (£2.1 trillion)**!

CRIMINAL CAREERS
ROGUES AND ROBBERS

Criminal schemes to get rich quick don't always go according to plan...

In 2008, in Bristol, UK, a clueless crook spotted a car with a state-of-the-art sat nav. He smashed into it, unaware of the **internal camera** which recorded images of a tattoo on his neck which featured the thief's **name** and **date of birth**.

The following year, in Iowa, USA, two bumbling men broke into a home, having disguised themselves with false beards and glasses scribbled on with a **permanent pen**. When the police tracked down their getaway car, the wannabe criminal masterminds were still covered in ink.

Two easy-peasy arrests for the cops!

Try them in a pasta sauce!

Great idea!

ONE FOR THE SNIFFER DOGS

On an Austrian motorway, the police were alerted to an overpowering stink coming from three overloaded vans. Five smelly suspects were swiftly arrested for making off with 9.5 tonnes (10.5 tons) of **stolen garlic** – the weight of three average **hippos**!

FASHION FIASCO
FANCY AND FEATHERBRAINED

Huge and elaborate wigs were all the rage in the 18th century. They were constructed from human, horse, or goat hair, then powdered with animal fat, flour, chalk, clay, and perfume.

This made them **highly flammable** at a time when banquets and balls were lit by candles and heated by roaring fires.

Apparently, in 1778, a woman took shelter under a tree in St. James's Park, London, proudly sporting a colossal wig held up with long wire pins. Unfortunately, a storm started and the pins attracted the lightning. Her precious hairpiece was set on fire, leaving her with charred, singed stubble!

WELL-KEPT WIGS

The layers of powder, grease, and sweat made it hard to keep the fancy wigs clean, and they were a thriving habitat for armies of **lice**.

For those who could afford it, their repugnant hairpieces would be sent round to a **wigmaker** to be thoroughly boiled and deloused!

SWEET STALL
TOXIC TREATS

In the 1850s, William Hardaker, known as **Humbug Billy**, sold sweets at a market in Bradford, UK. On one occasion, he took his usual delivery of yummy peppermint humbugs to the market, but was unaware that this batch was different...

Sugar was incredibly expensive at this time, so sweet makers padded out the sweets with a powder known as "**daft**". This was a blend of limestone and plaster of Paris. A catastrophic mistake meant that instead of daft, an identical (but highly poisonous) white powder called **arsenic** had been used.

It had a devastating effect on the unsuspecting customers that had digested these humbugs, and led to a change in the law about **ingredients** that were allowed in food production.

I hope they don't "wine" about this batch!

BAD BREWERIES

The ancient Romans made a syrup called "**sapa**" by boiling grape juice in lead pots. The makers believed that the lead that dripped into the bubbling mix added sweetness and killed any bacteria. But in actual fact, it caused lead poisoning, especially among the wealthy, wine-drinking Roman elite!

TELEPHONE TECH
I'LL PUT YOU ON HOLD

When Alexander Graham Bell invented the telephone in 1876, he offered to sell his ground-breaking invention to **Western Union**, a powerful company that dominated telegraph communication. But Western Union turned down his $100,000 price tag with the opinion that his telephone was "hardly more than a toy" and "of no use to us".

By 1900, the Bell Company was huge, and almost **600,000** telephones were in use!

Just 14,999,998 to go!

HORSE POWER

Henry Ford offered his lawyer, Horace Rackham, a chance to invest in the **Ford Motor Company** in 1903. Horace's bank manager warned him off, advising that, "The horse is here to stay, but the automobile is only a novelty – a fad!" By 1927, more than **15 million Ford Model Ts** had been sold, so it was lucky that Horace ignored his bank manager!

FIRST RATE FAILURES
CEREAL INVESTORS

Business leaders are often great at learning from their mistakes, and **William Keith Kellogg** is no exception.

In 1894, William and his older brother John revolutionized breakfasts forever. They were testing ways to create a digestible bread substitute and accidentally left a batch of boiled wheat sitting out overnight. When they pressed it, rolled it out, and toasted it, **cornflakes** were born!

The cereal is now sold in over **100** countries.

A SAUCE SENSATION

In the 1830s, two chemists, **John Lea** and **William Perrins**, were asked to recreate a spicy Indian sauce. Their first batch tasted foul, so they left it in a cellar and forgot about it. Fast forward 18 months and it had fermented into the glorious, tangy **Worcestershire sauce** we love today!

Chapter 7
GEOGRAPHICAL GAFFES

Page 59	Map Mishaps
Page 60	Double Deal
Page 61	A Frosty Fee
Page 62	Erik the Red
Page 63	Abel Tasman
Page 64	Italy Invades
Page 65	Sat Nav Slip-ups
Page 66	Antarctica
Page 67	Columbus
Page 68	Westerly Wind
Page 69	Lightning Strikes

Just turn left at the next cactus!

MAP MISHAPS
PERPLEXING PLANS

Pioneering **cartographers** have made some epic slip-ups with their map making. Let's dive into some of their major blunders...

In the 15th century, European explorers landed on the other side of the Atlantic. Now known as the Americas, the massive scale of this land was causing mapmakers to scratch their heads as they tried to reproduce the geography accurately. Early maps, up until the 1700s, showed part of **California** as a separate island, often complete with **sea monsters** for fun!

Similarly, the "Mountains of Kong" were a mythical mountain range in **West Africa** that appeared on maps from 1798. This feature was made up by overenthusiastic European cartographers, who were finally corrected by explorer Louis Binger in 1889.

They must be around here somewhere!

POLAR PLANS

The oldest known map featuring **Antarctica** was drawn up by the Turkish cartographer **Piri Reis** in 1513 CE. The amazing accuracy of this map baffles historians, since Antarctica wasn't officially discovered until 1820!

DOUBLE DEAL
THE LOUISIANA PURCHASE

Show me the money!

Napoleon Bonaparte, the legendary French leader, was constantly waging wars on unsuspecting territories, so he was often desperate for cash. France claimed ownership of a huge portion of North America, stretching from the Mississippi River to the Rocky Mountains, and Napolean offered to sell it to the US.

Thomas Jefferson, the US president at the time, snatched up this deal for just $15 million (£11 million) in 1803, doubling the size of the USA. This gave him control of the crucial trading port of New Orleans, access to huge tracts of farming land, and valuable natural resources.

A DEVASTATING DEAL

The Louisiana Purchase was **devastating** for hundreds of thousands of Native Americans. They were brutally forced from their **ancestral lands**, with many not surviving the journey.

A FROSTY FEE
THE USA BUYS ALASKA

Russia claimed **Alaska** in 1799, but found this far-flung territory a nightmare to manage and make profitable.

The solution? The **USA** checked their bank balance and offered Russia $7.2 million (£5.3 million) – an **absolute steal** at just two cents per acre!

But despite its huge size, US newspapers mocked the deal, dismissing Alaska as a barren, frozen **wasteland** with zero profit potential. Still, the deal was signed and sealed on 30 March 1867.

PROFIT OR LOSS?

The agreement became an epic fail for Russia and a jackpot for the USA. Alaska was bursting with **natural resources** including fur, timber, fish, gold, copper, and zinc. Today, the 49th state of the USA pumps out **400,000 barrels of oil** every single day – this comes at the expense of the **First Nations** who live there, as well as the environment.

ERIK THE RED
OR ERIK THE ESTATE AGENT

Meet **Erik the Red**, the Norse explorer. After getting booted out of **Iceland**, he sailed west for 1,000 km (600 miles) and stumbled across a mystery island.

Erik sneaked back to Iceland to urge others to join his wild adventure and help build a settlement on this brand-new colony. He called the island **Greenland** — a brilliant trick to make this frozen region sound lush and inviting!

Some Icelanders signed up, and in 985 CE he launched 25 ships packed with livestock, supplies, and 700 eager but anxious passengers. Despite 11 vessels getting shipwrecked, Erik and his family survived the crossing and set up his chieftain's power base in **Qassiarsuk**, southern Greenland.

Are we there yet?

FACT FILE

TRAVELLING TRIBE: Erik's son, Leif, is thought to have been the first European visitor to North America in 1000 CE, beating Christopher Columbus by 500 years!

GRAPES FOR GREENLAND: Leif's crew discovered an island bursting with wild grapes. They named the island **Vinland**, and sailed back to Greenland with their ship full of vines and grapes.

ABEL TASMAN
LAND AHOY

Abel Tasman was a Dutch seafarer, explorer, and navigation wizard! Unaware that it was inhabited, he was on a mission to discover the legendary southern continent, **Terra Australis**, and claim it for his bosses at the Dutch East India Company.

On 24 November 1642, he came across an island he named **Van Diemen's Land** (now called **Tasmania**, after the man himself!). He sailed east, and 20 days later spotted **New Zealand**, dubbing it **Staten Landt** (Land of the States).

After navigating the Indian Ocean, Abel not only failed to discover a new continent, he completely missed Australia — a land he had cruised tantalizingly close to!

An apple a day is the Tasmanian way!

FAST FACTS

EARLY DAYS: The ancestors of **Aboriginal Tasmanians** arrived from mainland Australia around 41,000 years ago, when sea levels were lower.

TAKE A BITE: Tasmania earned the nickname **Apple Isle** thanks to its legendary apple-growing industry.

ITALY INVADES
MAYHEM IN THE MOUNTAINS

In the 19th century, greedy European powers invaded and colonized many **African countries**, grabbing the riches and resources from this vast continent. Italy jumped headfirst into the "**Scramble for Africa**", too.

On 1 March 1896, 18,000 Italian troops were certain they would overtake the northeast African country of Ethiopia. This confidence was short-lived as the 100,000-strong Ethiopian force was equipped with cutting-edge guns supplied by European countries — including Italy!

The Italians planned a surprise attack over the mountains, but their maps were diabolical, and they got hopelessly lost in the brutal terrain. The muddled Italian soldiers got separated from their comrades, so Ethiopian forces simply picked off the enemy one-by-one. An Italian humiliation.

Mayday! Mayday!

DOCKED ON DRY LAND

Ships depend on their Automatic Identification System (AIS) for crucial location data. These systems aren't completely reliable though, and researchers proved this by hacking the ship *Eleanor Gordon*'s AIS. They switched its location from the Mississippi River to the middle of Texas — 2,000 km (1,200 miles) inland!

SAT NAV SLIP-UPS
DUD DIRECTIONS

Spare a thought for two tourists whose **sat nav** sent them (and their hire car) down a narrow footpath to St Catherine's Island, Wales, in 2023. The car got completely jammed, forcing the embarrassed holidaymakers to wriggle through the windows and catch a train to their hotel. The car stayed stuck for a week, with plans to chop it up and haul it out in pieces. Luckily, a super-strong device, called a **winch**, did the job and saved the brand-new car from the scrap heap!

That same year, a driver in Essex, UK, was faithfully following his sat nav when he noticed the steering felt odd. His car was almost entirely **underwater**, having motored down a track that ended in the River Chelmer rather than his chosen destination!

TAKING THE LONG WAY

In 2013, a Belgian woman embarked on a simple 80-km (50-mile) errand to collect a friend in Brussels. She got distracted while punching in her destination and ended up on a marathon **1,450-km (901-mile)** journey to Croatia! Despite five border crossings and several fuel stops, she just kept on driving. She finally made it home **60 hours** after her epic trip began!

ANTARCTICA
A SHARED CONTINENT

Although **Russian explorer** Fabian Gottlieb von Bellingshausen first spotted **Antarctica** in 1820, the **UK** swooped in to claim ownership of the frozen territory 88 years later. Since then, there has been a scramble of counterclaims from Argentina, Australia, Chile, France, New Zealand, and Norway. Could this showdown be settled with a speed skating race or snowman-building competition?

Well, that would have been fun, but instead they drafted **The Antarctic Treaty System**. This named the territory as a shared continent for peace and science, banning military acts, nuclear testing, and waste dumping schemes.

Well, it's all down to my thick layer of blubber...

ANTARCTIC RESEARCH

CLIMATE CHANGE: Researchers drill ice cores to understand past climates and the changes happening to our oceans and ice sheets.

ANIMAL SURVIVAL: Scientists study how land and sea species have adapted and thrived in the continent's freezing environment.

ASTRONOMY: The clear and stable atmosphere of Antarctica makes it a perfect location for exploring our universe.

COLUMBUS
THE ITALIAN EXPLORER

Christopher Columbus is known for **"discovering"** the Americas for Europeans to explore and later colonize. But overlooked for a long time was the devastating impact his voyages had on the **Indigenous Peoples** who already lived there, leading to violence, slavery, and the introduction of diseases that ravaged their communities.

Christopher was no mathematician, and he miscalculated **Earth's circumference** by a whopping **30%**. Using this dodgy data, he set sail in 1492, aiming for Asia. Two months later, he landed in the Bahamas – **12,000 km (7,500 miles)** off target! He stubbornly insisted he'd reached his destination, calling it the **West Indies**, and forced his crew to sign a document to swear they'd reached Asia. Christopher sailed on to **Cuba**, convinced it was mainland **China**. When he returned to Europe, he brought turkeys, pineapples, tobacco, gold, and, tragically, captured Indigenous People.

DEAR DIARY

Christopher's fascinating journals report the first encounters between his crew and Indigenous Peoples, the sailor's grumbles about grim conditions onboard, and his desperate attempts to wow **Spanish royalty** with treasure.

WESTERLY WIND
EXPLORER PEDRO ÁLVARES CABRAL

In March 1500, the Portuguese explorer **Pedro Álvares Cabral** launched an epic voyage to India, with 13 ships and a crew of 1,200. They sailed south-west past Africa's coastline, but then disaster struck...

Strong winds and currents took them way off course, dragging the entire fleet westward until they slammed into **Brazil**! Despite Indigenous Peoples like the **Tupi** and **Tapuia** already calling it home, Pedro claimed the territory for Portugal's crown, naming it the **Island of the True Cross**.

Over the next 300 years, they used forced labour and slavery to exploit the country's resources of brazilwood, sugar, gold, and diamonds.

Oi, Pedro! We were here first!

FAST FACTS

BAGS OF BEANS: Brazil is the world's largest coffee grower! Almost 4 million tonnes (4.4 million tons) are produced each year – the weight of 9,300 jumbo jets!

WILD WATERWAY: Northern Brazil is dominated by the **Amazon River**, stretching an incredible **6,840 km (4,250 miles)**. That's like hiking from London to Edinburgh and back, five times!

LIGHTNING STRIKES
WHAT A LUCKY STREAK

Let's meet an extreme weather winner! US Park Ranger Roy Sullivan was hit by **lightning** an unbelievable **seven times** — and he survived every single one!

Between 1942 and 1977, this storm superhero lost a big toenail, eyebrows, and eyelashes. He was also knocked out cold, suffered burns to his chest and shoulder, his hair caught fire (twice), he injured his ankle, and he went deaf in one ear.

Roy dodged an eighth strike when a storm rolled in while he was enjoying some family time in his back garden. The lightning missed him — but struck his **wife** instead!

I should have worn a hard hat!

EXTREME WEATHER

The world's most spectacular **lightning strike** stretched 768 km (477 miles) over the US states of Mississippi, Louisiana, and Texas — that's 86 times the height of Mount Everest! Meanwhile, in Bangladesh, the heaviest hailstone ever recorded tipped the scales at **1.02 kg (2.25 lb)** — equivalent to 22 golf balls.

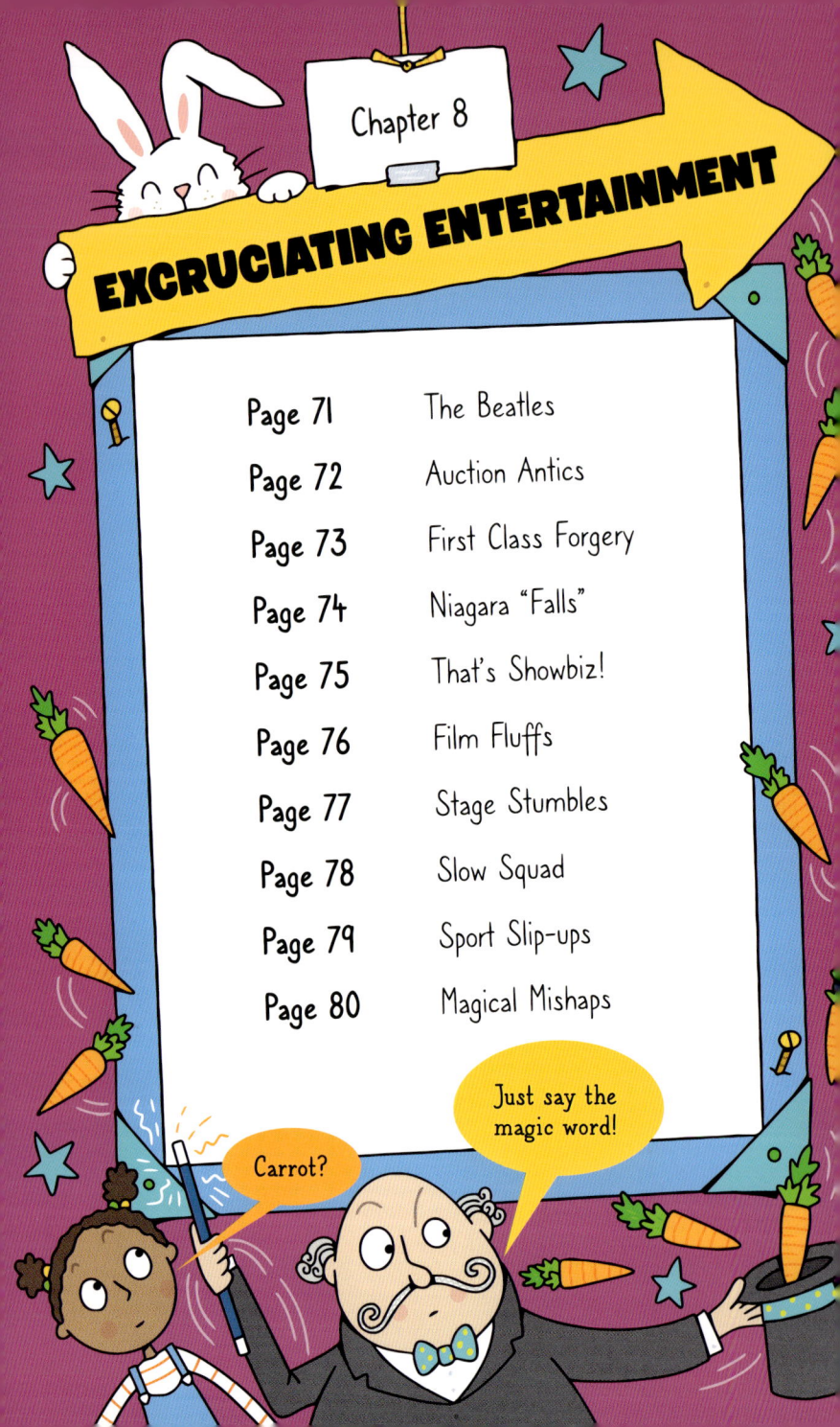

THE BEATLES
CAN'T BUY ME A CONTRACT

In 1960, four friends from Liverpool, UK, formed a band. They refined their sound at the local Cavern Club, and then spent five months gigging in Hamburg, Germany.

Desperate for a record deal, these determined dreamers, now known as **The Beatles**, drove 10 hours through a snowstorm on New Year's Day 1962, to audition for Decca Records in London.

Dick Rowe, a record company bigwig, was unimpressed and made one of the world's most catastrophic commercial decisions. **"Guitar groups are on their way out"**, he allegedly told the disappointed foursome. Whoops! They went on to sell over 600 million records with rival record company, EMI.

Trust me! The next big thing is the recorder.

DICK ROWE

TOP TUNES

In April 1964, The Beatles held the top five slots in the American music charts! They scored 19 number one albums in the USA, and 15 in the UK.

46 years later, The Beatles made it onto Apple iTunes. Week one results? Only 450,000 albums and two million songs downloaded...

AUCTION ANTICS
PROFITS IN PAINTING

A painting called **Salvator Mundi** was auctioned in 1958 for a measly £45. Snooty art experts had dubbed it a knockoff **Leonardo da Vinci** – the genius who painted the Mona Lisa.

Salvator Mundi vanished for almost 50 years before popping up at a Louisiana auction. The price had leapt to $10,000 (£7,300) but the new owners had a hunch – was there more to this painting than previously thought?

They splashed some cash on meticulous restoration, peeling away layers of "overpainting" and centuries of dirt. Their gamble paid off. Experts confirmed it was a long-lost Leonardo da Vinci **masterpiece**, once part of the Queen of England's collection in the 1600s. In 2017, it was sold for a jaw-dropping $450.3 million (£333 million) – the **most expensive painting** ever sold!

So, the hip bone's connected to the thigh bone?

FAST FACTS

AHEAD OF HIS TIME: Leonardo da Vinci's notebooks feature mind-blowing designs for helicopters, hang gliders, submarines, and armoured tanks!

BONE BOFFIN: Leonardo dissected over 30 corpses to master human anatomy.

FIRST CLASS FORGERY
DUTCH DOODLES

Artist Han van Meegeren was desperate — critics trashed his work and buyers avoided him like the plague.

He planned his revenge — he would forge a **Johannes Vermeer** painting (one of history's greatest Dutch painters) and trick those snooty art critics. Once the experts praised the fake, he would publicly humiliate them by revealing the hoax!

His 1934 "Vermeer" was flawless. Han used an authentic old canvas and 17th century paints mixed with a material called **Bakelite**, which aged the painting to perfection. Critics hailed it as a masterpiece, so Han scrapped his original revenge plan and launched a lucrative fake-Vermeer empire!

He raked in millions, even conning Nazi leader **Hermann Göring** out of 1.65 million guilders (£650,000) during WWII.

You've been framed!

FROM TREASON TO FRAUD

After WWII, Han van Meegeren was arrested for selling **Dutch treasures** to the Nazis. Faced with a death sentence, he confessed — the painting was fake! To prove it, authorities forced him to paint another forgery in his prison cell. He aced the test and received a **one-year** sentence for fraud.

NIAGARA "FALLS"
TAKING THE PLUNGE

Thrill-seekers have been launching themselves over **Niagara Falls** for over a century — with mixed results. In 1901, fearless **Annie Edson Taylor** made attempt number one, surviving the drop in a wooden barrel. She tested her contraption's strength beforehand — by sending over a cat!

Ten years later, daredevil **Bobby Leach** crossed it off his bucket list, although his endeavour did land him with two shattered kneecaps and a mangled jaw.

In 1920, **Charles Stephens** gave it a shot, in a barrel with an **anvil** tied to his feet and straps to support his arms. As his cask hit the base of the falls, the anvil torpedoed straight through the bottom. Charles disappeared, leaving his tattooed right arm still attached to the harness!

Break a leg!

ABSURD ATTEMPT

In 1990, Jesse Sharp tried riding over the falls in a **kayak**. Worried about ruining his appearance for promotional photos, he refused both **helmet** and **life jacket**. Safety crews knew nothing about Jesse's stunt, so weren't on hand to offer help. Reaching the falls' edge, Jesse triumphantly raised his paddle and disappeared into the raging water — gone forever.

THAT'S SHOWBIZ!
TERRIFYING TRANSMISSION

In 1938, CBS Radio Network broadcast an adaptation of H.G. Wells' **War of the Worlds** — a tale of a brutal Martian invasion of Earth, narrated by young hotshot **Orson Welles**.

Orson read the book in a realistic "breaking news" format, and countless panicky listeners actually **believed** that the story of **aliens** destroying the planet with gas and heat rays was real. There were stories of widespread alarm and panic. Reports described people fleeing their homes, churches crammed with praying congregations, and emergency services flooded with frantic calls. In Grovers Mill, USA, terrified residents opened fire on the town's water tower, mistaking it for an alien's **"tripod machine"**!

Orson apologized, but his hoax catapulted him to international stardom and earned him a wealthy **radio sponsor**!

No news is good news, right?

THE SOUND OF SILENCE

On 18 April 1930, BBC Radio's **news announcer** memorably declared: "Good evening. There is no news". Rather than stuff the 15 minutes with dull stories or irrelevant information, they played **soothing music** instead!

FILM FLUFFS
CINEMATIC CLANGERS

The 1959 film **Plan 9 From Outer Space** is legendary – for being spectacularly awful! Its cemetery location featured gravestones that wobbled like flimsy cardboard, and there were scene changes that went from day to night and back again, mid-dialogue!

UFOs looked suspiciously like **hubcaps** dangling on string, and when a film star sadly died mid-shoot, he was replaced by a taller, younger actor holding a cape over his face to disguise the switch!

A planet was clearly an **inflatable toy**, the camera operator's loud footsteps echoed during quiet scenes, and a danger-loving "detective" absent-mindedly scratched his head – with a **loaded gun**!

STAR QUALITY

Before **George Lucas** directed the first **Star Wars** film he struck a deal with **20th Century Fox** – he'd trade his $500,000 (£370,000) salary for the rights to **merchandise** and **make sequels**. The Star Wars franchise went on to bank around $20 billion (£14.8 billion).

STAGE STUMBLES
MUSICAL MUDDLES

At the 2013 **Billboard Music Awards**, singer Miguel's spectacular moment went hilariously wrong when he mistimed his stage-to-stage leap, accidentally hitting one audience member on the head and walloping another fan's arm. Two years later, one bruised showgoer sued for compensation!

During U2's 2015 tour, guitarist **The Edge** took an epic tumble off the stage in Vancouver. The band played on, while security guards hauled him back to his feet. He later posted a picture of his grazed arm, with the caption **"Didn't see the edge"**!

It's "times like these" I need a plaster cast!

FOO FACTS

That same year, Foo Fighters were mid-song in Sweden when frontman **Dave Grohl** slipped and crashed into the crowd. Clutching his microphone, he told fans, "I think I just **broke my leg**. I'm gonna go to the **hospital** but I'll be right back!" He raced back with his leg in a cast and finished the show – performing from a throne! Rock royalty!

SLOW SQUAD
BETTER LATE THAN NEVER

On 27 April 1908, the international teams were parading at **London's Summer Olympics** opening ceremony. For the first time ever, athletes were marching proudly behind their nation's flags, but wait... where was **Russia**? What was the hold-up?

Plot twist: while the rest of the world had embraced the newfangled **Gregorian calendar**, the Russian Empire was still clinging to the old **Julian calendar** (and didn't make the switch for another ten years).

This mix-up meant their bewildered team rocked up **12 days** late! When the Russians finally showed up, their athletes got their own special parade, and ended up winning a gold for figure skating and two wrestling silvers!

We'd better get our skates on!

ROGUE REFEREES

In the 1972 **Olympic men's basketball final**, the USA grabbed a 50-49 lead over the USSR. The last three seconds of the match were replayed over and over, with chaotic interventions from officials. After botched clock resets, the USSR scored, snatching victory by one point. Furious USA players **boycotted** their silver medals entirely!

SPORT SLIP-UPS
BALL GAME BLUNDERS

In 2015, champion skier **Marcel Hirscher** was very close to being hit by a camera drone during a vital slalom race. The terrifying near miss prompted the **International Ski Federation** to ban drones from World Cup events for almost a decade!

Newly married football midfielder **Paulo Diogo** was less fortunate in 2004, when he celebrated his team's goal by leaping on a fence to salute ecstatic fans. Joy soon turned to horror when his wedding ring snagged a barrier and his finger got **completely severed**. Stewards searched desperately for the missing digit, while the irritated referee **booked** a distraught Paulo for excessive celebration time!

Gimme a D...gimme an R...gimme an O!

FOOTIE FACTS

Italian team Dro's **goalkeeper**, Loris Angeli, suffered huge embarrassment during a penalty shoot out in 2011. An opposing Termeno player smashed his shot against the crossbar and Loris sprinted towards his triumphant teammates. Behind him, the ball dropped from the crossbar, spun, and gradually crawled towards the goal mouth, stopping just **inside the goal**! The final result? Termeno 5 – Dro 4. This caused **pandemonium**...

MAGICAL MISHAPS
ABRACA-DON'T-DON'T

Magician William Ellsworth Robinson's signature trick was his death-defying **"Bullet Catch"** illusion. A nervous assistant would blast a gun at the showman, and William would pluck a bullet from mid-air — sometimes with his teeth! His secret? A cleverly rigged gun firing harmless **blanks**.

One fateful night in 1918, the magician failed to inspect the gun and it accidently fired a **real** bullet. This put William in the company of 11 other magicians who fatally fluffed the "bullet catch" trick (so don't try this at home!).

Karr the Magician's heart-stopping stunt involved escaping from a straitjacket while a car sped towards him. In 1930, Karr misjudged his timing and got flattened!

Shall we edit that bit out?

NAILING THE TRICK

During a live broadcast in Poland in 2016, a TV presenter took part in a magician's trick which involved **slamming** her hand onto four paper bags — with one of them hiding a sharp nail. On the first smash, the nail pierced straight through her hand! Shocked viewers watched the traumatized presenter collapse in agony, with the nail **still impaled**. Later, the TV star was filmed insisting that she was **totally fine!**